Old King Cole ☆ Doctor Foster ☆ Cool Queen Wenceslas
Humpty Dumpty ☆ Bendy Burglar ☆ Incey Wincey ☆ Silly Sand Man

If you're very bored indeed,
Here's some stuff for you to read:

This magnificent little book was
published by those CHARMING people at

ORCHARD BOOKS

who all live together at:

96 Leonard Street, London EC2A 4XD

(You can send them a Christmas card if you like.)

Published down under by

32/45-51 Huntley Street, Alexandria, NSW 2015

Orchard Books Australia

First published in Great Britain in 2002. First paperback edition 2003

Blah, blah, blahdy blah...

Text © Laurence Anholt 2002

Arthur's drawings:
HANDS OFF!

Don't steal the
words, man.

Illustrations © Arthur Robins 2002

The rights of Laurence Anholt to be identified as the author and
Arthur Robins as the illustrator of this work have been asserted by them
in accordance with the Copyright, Designs and Patents Act, 1998.

Dooby dooby dooby doo..

A CIP catalogue record for this book is available from the British Library.

etc, etc...

Does anyone read this stuff?

ISBN 1 84121 012 9 (hardback)
ISBN 1 84121 020 X (paperback)

1 3 5 7 9 10 8 6 4 2 (hardback)
1 3 5 7 9 10 8 6 4 2 (paperback)

ARE YOU STILL THERE?

Printed in Great Britain

Goodnight.

Really Frilly

YUM!

Sam the Man ☆ Johnny Stout ☆ Little Bo-Peep ☆ The Queen
Mary, Mary ☆ The Deadly Dinner Ladies ☆ Greedy Green Martian

✬ CONTENTS ✬

MARY HAD A DINOSAUR

Mary had a dinosaur
Fifty metres wide,
And everywhere that Mary went
It followed by her side.

It came with her to school one day,
The kids began to clap.
They'd never seen a dinosaur
Sit on teacher's lap.

The dinosaur said, "Listen, kids,
Today I'm taking school.
We'll do some *Seriously Silly Rhymes.*"
And the children shouted "COOL!"

KING COLE'S GOAL

Old King Cole
Played in goal
But a really bad goalie was he.
He booted the ball
Right over a wall
And ten miles out to sea.

Now every ref he has a whistle
And blows as loud as can be.
So Old King Cole came out of goal
And tickled the referee.

SQUIRMY WORM SONG

To market, to market to buy a fat
worm,
Home again, home again, squirmity
squirm.

To market to market, to take the
    worm back.
Hoi! Which is the front and which is
    the back?

Here is the answer to all of these
    riddles:

Tickle the middle and see which
    end giggles!

SING A SONG OF SWEETIES

Sing a song of sixpence,
A pocket full of treats.
I'd love a great big chocolate bar
And half a ton of sweets.

When the sweets are eaten,
My tummy will be sore,
So I'll hurry to the sweetie shop
And buy myself some more.

This poem contains no
artificial flavourings.

BENDY BURGLAR

There was a crooked man
Who robbed a crooked bank,

And made a crooked getaway
In a crooked army tank.

They called a crooked cop,
Out of his crooked shower,

Who chased the crooked burglar
At ninety miles an hour.

Down a crooked hill,

They hit a crooked truck,

Which straightened out the crooked
man.

What a crooked bit of luck!

PUNKY SKUNK

Tom, Tom, short-sighted punk
Stole a mole and away did bunk.
Boy, that mole, he really stunk.

I ain't no mole, I'm a stinky skunk!

BEEHIVE YOURSELF

A fellow named Sunny Magee
Was stung on the bum by a bee.
Sunny said,

Honey,
That really ain't funny.
Now buzz off and just let me be.

JACK'S SNACKS

Jack Sprat is awful fat,
His wife is even fatter.
Their favourite meal
Is elephant seal,
Deep-fried with chips in batter.

This poem contains 9,900,078 calories

SHARK ATTACK

One, two, three, four, five,
Once I caught a shark alive.

Six, seven, eight, nine, ten,
Then I threw him back again.

Why did you set him free?
Because he started eating me.

Which section did he eat?
From my neck down to my feet.

SILLY SAND MAN

Hush-a-bye, Daddy, asleep on the
  beach.
When the tide comes, then Daddy
will screech.
When Daddy screeches, we'll each
  give a hand
To dig poor old Daddy out of the
  sand.

A DINO SAW US

Jack and Jill went up the hill
To fetch a brontosaurus.
They couldn't wait to find a mate
For their tiny tyrannosaurus.

They heard a roar from the mighty jaw
Of something quite enormous.
"Run back!" said Jack. "I will," said Jill,

I wonder if he saw us?

"Relax," said Jack, "it won't attack.
They're strictly herbivorous."
(But Jill and Jack became a snack
For a monster megalosaurus.)

SOME WORDS ABOUT BIRDS

Two little dicky birds,
Sitting on a tree.
One like you,
One like me.

I am the pretty one,
The ugly one is you,
Just like a dodo
Escaped from a zoo.

PAT-A-POEM

Pat-a-cake, pat-a-cake, baker's man,
Bake me a cake as fast as you can.
Are you aware of the time you'd save,
If you upgraded to a microwave?

PING!

SAM THE MAN

A surfer named Sam from Waikiki
Said,

I'm tough and I'm tanned and I'm freaky.

He wasn't so brave
When a huge tidal wave
Made him exceedingly peaky.

POLLY PUT THE TELLY ON

Polly put the telly on,
Polly put the telly on,
Polly put the telly on,
On top of her head.

Sukey put the toaster on,
Sukey put the toaster on,
Sukey put the toaster on,
On top of the bread.

Wally took his wellies off,
Wally took his wellies off,
Wally took his wellies off,
To stop them getting wet.

Nicky took her knickers down,
Nicky took her knickers down,
Nicky took her knickers down,
To the launderette.

MOOSE ON THE LOOSE

Hickory, dickory, dock.

A moose ran up my frock.

I gave a cough,

My frock fell off,
Hickory, dickory, dock.

DEADLY DINNER LADIES

Who killed young Robin?
I, said the dinner lady,

Who else is dead?
Asked the school Head,
Trembling with dread,

We all will die,
I replied with a sigh,
For we all ate the pie,

All the teachers of the school
Started wailing and a-yelping,
For they all had eaten
A big second helping.

A LEPRACHAUN ON THE LAWN

A short and pointless verse.

Round and round the garden like a leprechaun. One step, two step, digging up the lawn.

PC POEM

Girls and boys sit down to play,
Computers glow as bright as day.
Leave your homework and leave
    your tea,
It's far more fun on my PC.

SCRUB-A-DUB-DUB

Rub-a-dub, dub,
There's a sub in my tub,
Floating about with ease.
I only hope that periscope
Won't peep between my knees.

ALL ABOUT
THE AUTHOR

Laurence Anholt lives right here:
But sometimes goes abroad.
He writes those Seriously Silly books
(Which won that big award.*)

He drives a little Beetle car
With daring and great skill.
He likes to climb up apple trees
Because he gets a thrill.

He has three children, here they are:
And who else shares his life?
This lady's name is Catherine,
His lovely, darling wife.

LAURENCE'S CHILDREN

* Smarties Gold Award

ALL ABOUT
THE ILLUSTRATOR

Arthur Robins gets up late
And walks his tiny poodle.
He wears his trousers inside out
And his favourite word is "noodle".

He used to ride a motorbike
When he was young and free.
But now he rides a lawnmower,
And drinks a lot of tea.

He has two girls who look like this:
His wife's name is Elaine.
This diagram will illustrate
The inside of his brain.

ARTHUR'S
CHILDREN

ARTHUR'S
WIFE

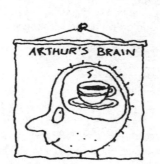

ARTHUR'S BRAIN

SERIOUSLY SILLY RHYMES and STORIES

Laurence Anholt ☆ Arthur Robins

All priced at £3.99

Seriously Silly books are available from all good bookshops,
or can be ordered direct from the publisher:
Orchard Books, PO BOX 29, Douglas IM99 1BQ
Credit card orders please telephone 01624 836000
or fax 01624 837033
or e-mail: bookshop@enterprise.net for details.

To order please quote title, author and ISBN
and your full name and address.
Cheques and postal orders should be
made payable to 'Bookpost plc'.

Postage and packing is FREE within the UK
(overseas customers should add £1.00 per book).

Prices and availability are subject to change.